Juneteenth
Celebrates Freedom

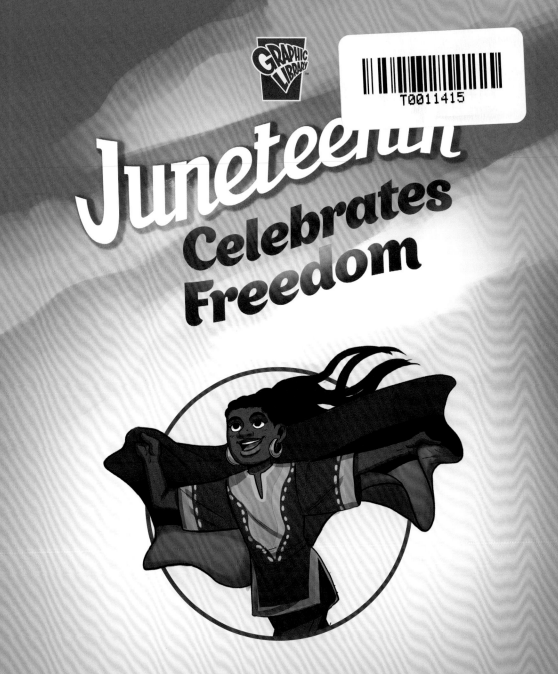

written by **Myra Faye Turner**
illustrated by **Markia Jenai**

CAPSTONE PRESS
a capstone imprint

Published by Capstone Press, an imprint of Capstone
1710 Roe Crest Drive, North Mankato, Minnesota 56003
capstonepub.com

Library of Congress Cataloging-in-Publication Data
Names: Turner, Myra Faye, author. | Jenai, Markia, illustrator.
Title: Juneteenth celebrates freedom / by Myra Faye Turner ; illustrated by Markia Jenai.
Description: North Mankato, Minnesota : Capstone Press, an imprint of Capstone, [2024] | Series: Great moments in history | Includes bibliographical references. | Audience: Ages 8 to 11 | Audience: Grades 4–6 | Summary: "In 1863, the Emancipation Proclamation declared that all enslaved people in Confederate States were legally free. But word traveled slowly during the Civil War. It wasn't until June 19, 1865—more than two months after the war ended—that the good news finally reached Galveston, Texas. From that moment forward, June 19 became a day to celebrate freedom—first in Texas and then across the country. How did Juneteenth develop over time, and what is the holiday's enduring legacy? Find out in an easy-to-read graphic novel that reveals why Juneteenth's evolution into a federal holiday is among the greatest moments in history"—Provided by publisher.
Identifiers: LCCN 2022047847 (print) | LCCN 2022047848 (ebook) | ISBN 9781669016977 (hardcover) | ISBN 9781669016922 (paperback) | ISBN 9781669016939 (ebook pdf) | ISBN 9781669016953 (kindle edition) | ISBN 9781669016960 (epub)
Subjects: LCSH: Juneteenth—Juvenile literature. | Slaves—Emancipation—Texas—Juvenile literature. | African Americans—Anniversaries, etc—Juvenile literature. | Slaves—Emancipation—United States—Juvenile literature.
Classification: LCC E185.93.T4 T87 2024 (print) | LCC E185.93.T4 (ebook) | DDC 394.263—dc23/eng/20221005
LC record available at https://lccn.loc.gov/2022047847
LC ebook record available at https://lccn.loc.gov/2022047848

Editorial Credits
Editor: Christopher Harbo; Designer: Tracy Davies; Production Specialist: Katy LaVigne

All internet sites appearing in back matter were available and accurate when this book was sent to press.

Direct quotations appear in bold italicized text on the following pages:
Page 5, from "Transcript of the Proclamation" (archives.gov, 2017).
Page 15, from "National Archives Safeguards Original 'Juneteenth' General Order" (archives.gov, 2020).
Page 24, from "The Real Opal Lee: Dear President Obama" (opalswalk2dc.com).
Page 25, from "The Mission of Opal Lee, Fort Worth's Grandmother of Juneteenth" by Jessica B. Harris (Southern Living, July 6, 2022).
Page 26, from "Remarks by President Biden at Signing of the Juneteenth National Independence Day Act" (whitehouse.gov, June 17, 2021).
Page 26, from @therealopallee (twitter.com, June 17, 2021).

Printed and bound in China 5379

Table of Contents

Introduction
The Middle Passage 4

Chapter 1
Emancipation 6

Chapter 2
The First Celebration 12

Chapter 3
Juneteenth Evolves 16

Chapter 4
Becoming an Official Federal Holiday 22

More About Juneteenth 28

Glossary... 30

Read More 31

Internet Sites.................................... 31

About the Author............................... 32

About the Illustrator 32

Beginning in 1525, millions of African men, women, and children were taken from their homes and families. They were brought to the Americas against their will.

The Middle Passage

For almost 350 years, white people enslaved Black people, forcing them to work for no pay. In the United States, most worked on plantations in the South.

The United States ended the African slave trade in 1808. However, slavery didn't end. Black people who were already on U.S. soil continued to be enslaved.

Throughout the history of slavery, some Black and white people pushed for freedom, or emancipation, for enslaved people. But others, mainly in the South, wanted to keep Black people enslaved.

We need a break.

Keep working until I tell you to stop.

Conflict between the northern and southern states increased after President Abraham Lincoln was elected in 1860.

Lincoln opposed slavery, but he felt it should end gradually. He also didn't want slavery to spread to the North. Still, white people in the South felt Lincoln's election signaled an immediate end to their free labor.

By February 1, 1861, seven pro-slavery states left the Union. They formed a new government and called themselves the Confederate States of America. They elected Jefferson Davis as their president.

UNION

CONFEDERACY

Then, on April 12, 1861, the split between the Union and the Confederacy ignited the Civil War (1861–1865). Four more states joined the Confederacy after the war started.

In September 1862, long before the war ended, President Lincoln made a bold military move. He issued the Emancipation Proclamation. This document did not free all enslaved people. Instead, it freed only those living in any Confederate state that refused to stop fighting and rejoin the Union by January 1, 1863.

. . . all persons held as slaves within any State or designated part of a State, the people whereof shall then be in rebellion against the United States, shall be then, thenceforward, and forever free . . .

Although Lincoln didn't have direct power to free people who were no longer under Union control, he encouraged Black people to leave Confederate states. He also asked Black men to join the Union army and navy.

News about freedom began spreading by word of mouth and by Union soldiers. In January 1863, enslaved people who learned they were free began leaving plantations.

But news traveled slower in those days. While some celebrated . . .

. . . many folks in states farther south didn't hear the news.

Meanwhile, the Civil War raged on for two more years. Then, on April 9, 1865, the Union won the war when Confederate General Robert E. Lee surrendered to Union General Ulysses S. Grant in Virginia.

Still, word of the Emancipation Proclamation hadn't yet reached everyone. In fact, it took two and a half more years for news of freedom to finally reach Texas.

Why did it take so long for the news to arrive? Some claim the first messenger was murdered as he galloped to Texas.

Others say white enslavers knew but wanted to keep it a secret for as long as they could.

Let's not tell them until after the harvest.

The longer they work, the better for us.

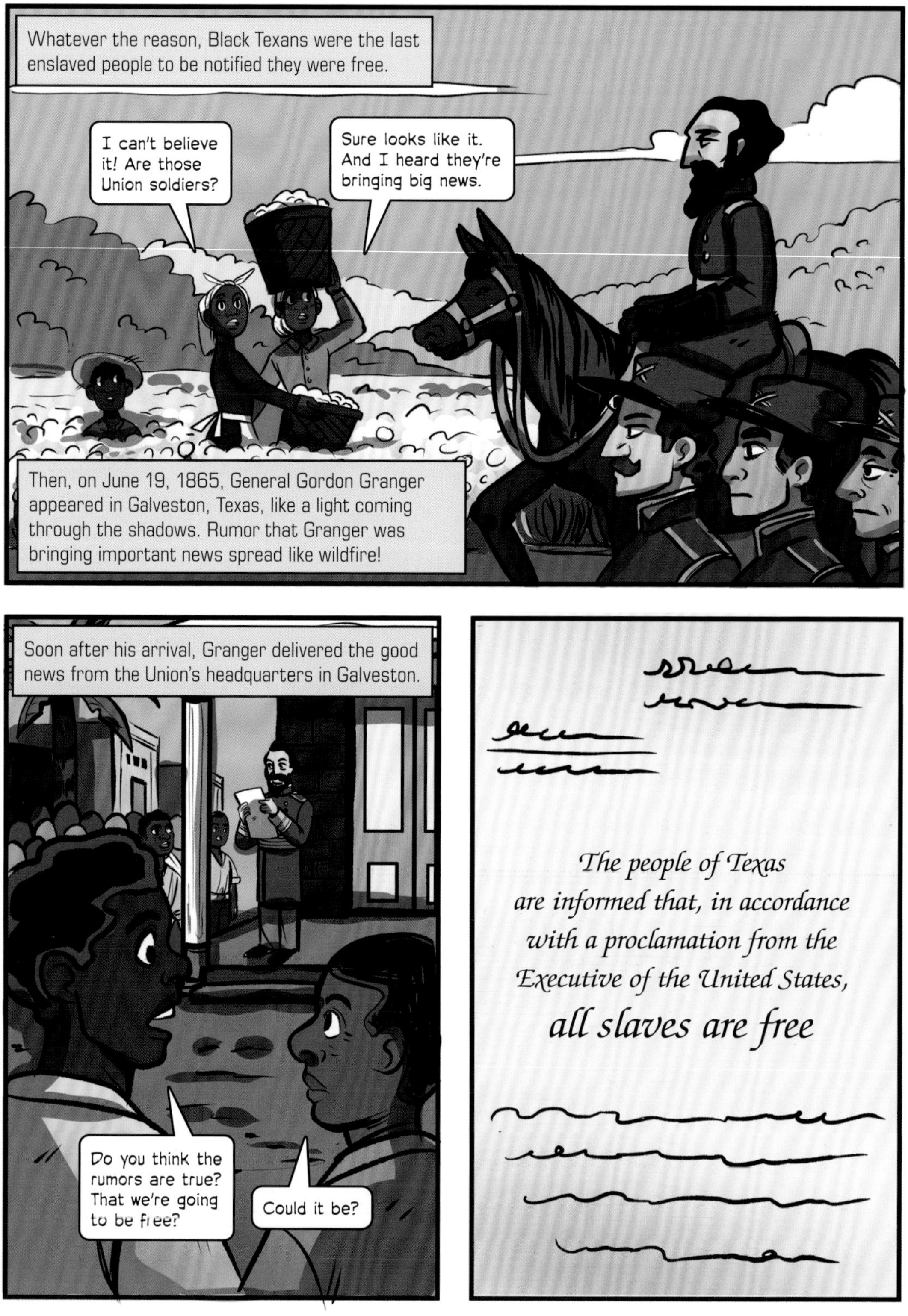
Whatever the reason, Black Texans were the last enslaved people to be notified they were free.
I can't believe it! Are those Union soldiers?
Sure looks like it. And I heard they're bringing big news.
Then, on June 19, 1865, General Gordon Granger appeared in Galveston, Texas, like a light coming through the shadows. Rumor that Granger was bringing important news spread like wildfire!
Soon after his arrival, Granger delivered the good news from the Union's headquarters in Galveston.
Do you think the rumors are true? That we're going to be free?
Could it be?
The people of Texas are informed that, in accordance with a proclamation from the Executive of the United States, all slaves are free

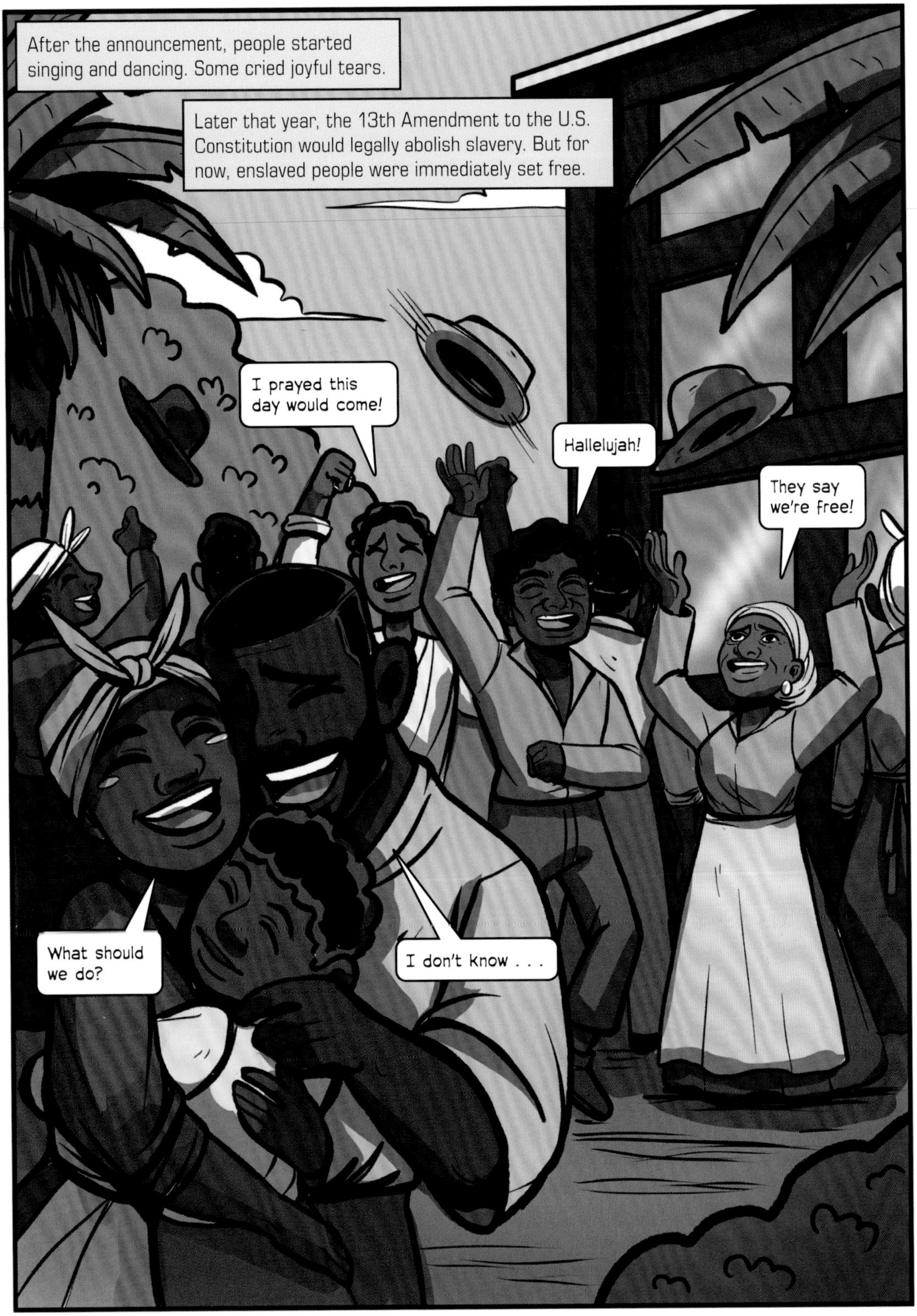
After the announcement, people started singing and dancing. Some cried joyful tears.
Later that year, the 13th Amendment to the U.S. Constitution would legally abolish slavery. But for now, enslaved people were immediately set free.
I prayed this day would come!
Hallelujah!
They say we're free!
What should we do?
I don't know . . .

After gaining their freedom, many Black Americans left the plantations. Some went North, hoping for a better life. Others remained in the South, the only home they knew. Most didn't have money. And some had only the clothes on their back.

Where should we go?

We're free. We can go wherever we want.

But they had each other. They had their freedom.

Enslavers had separated families, selling them to different plantations like livestock. After emancipation, Black Americans searched for their family members.

I'm so glad I found you.

I thought I would never see you again.

Some found their loved ones. But many never saw their families again.

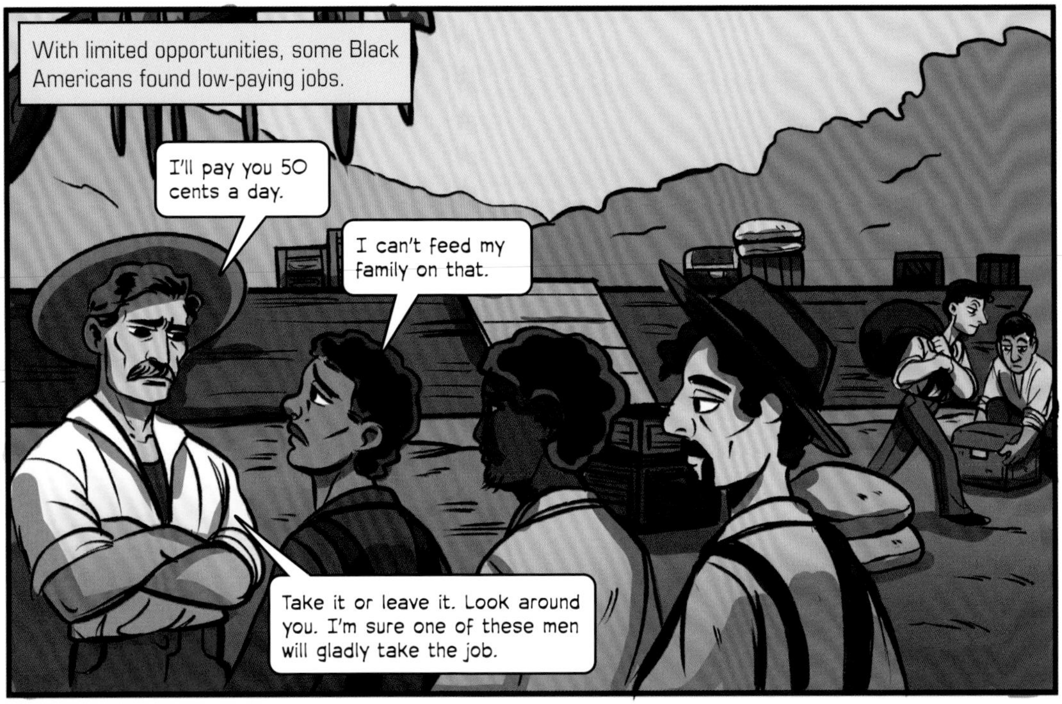
With limited opportunities, some Black Americans found low-paying jobs.
I'll pay you 50 cents a day.
I can't feed my family on that.
Take it or leave it. Look around you. I'm sure one of these men will gladly take the job.

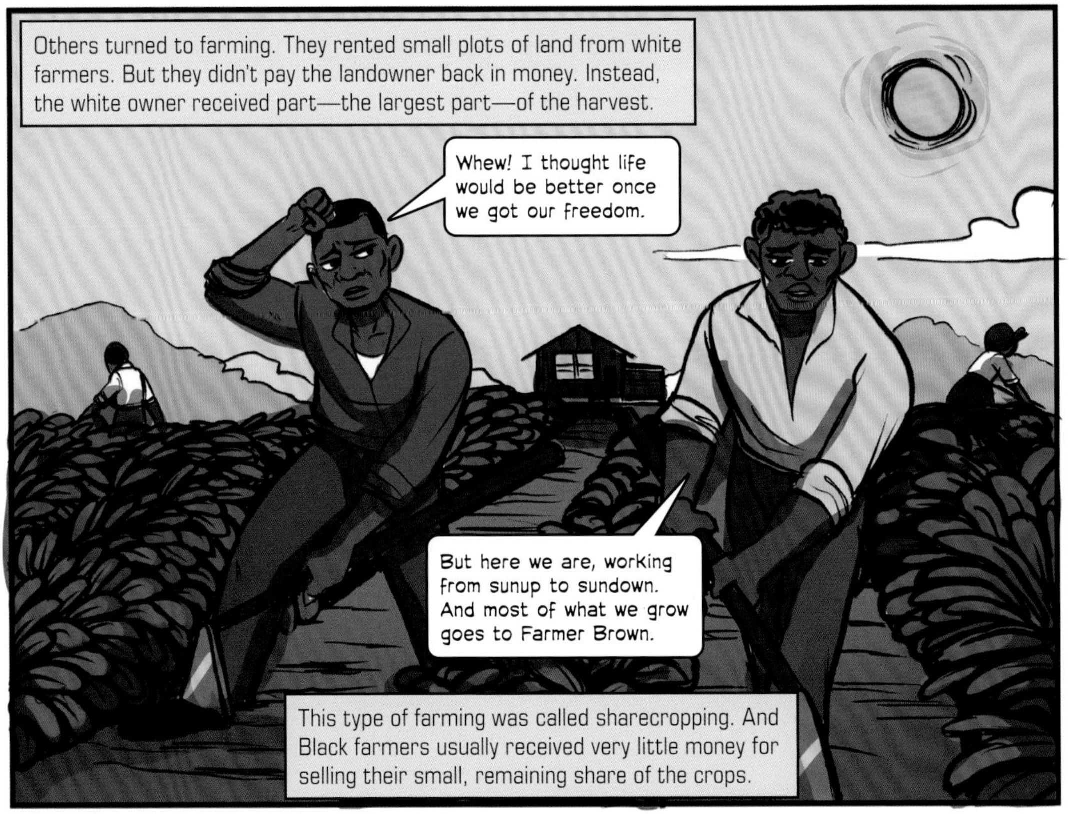
Others turned to farming. They rented small plots of land from white farmers. But they didn't pay the landowner back in money. Instead, the white owner received part—the largest part—of the harvest.
Whew! I thought life would be better once we got our freedom.
But here we are, working from sunup to sundown. And most of what we grow goes to Farmer Brown.
This type of farming was called sharecropping. And Black farmers usually received very little money for selling their small, remaining share of the crops.

JUNE 1866

19

Life was hard after the Civil War, but the good news Black Texans had received in Galveston was not forgotten. One year after Texans learned they were free, a celebration was held in Galveston.

The delightful sound of music and voices floated through the air.

From the beginning, food was a very important part of this celebration. Tables were stuffed with mouth-watering dishes.

And red-colored food—such as strawberries, red velvet cake, watermelon, barbecue, and red punch—were often on the menu.

I brought a cake. Made it from my grandmother's recipe.

Ooh! Red velvet. My favorite!

Why red? Some say red symbolized the blood of enslaved people who endured slavery and of those who lost their lives.

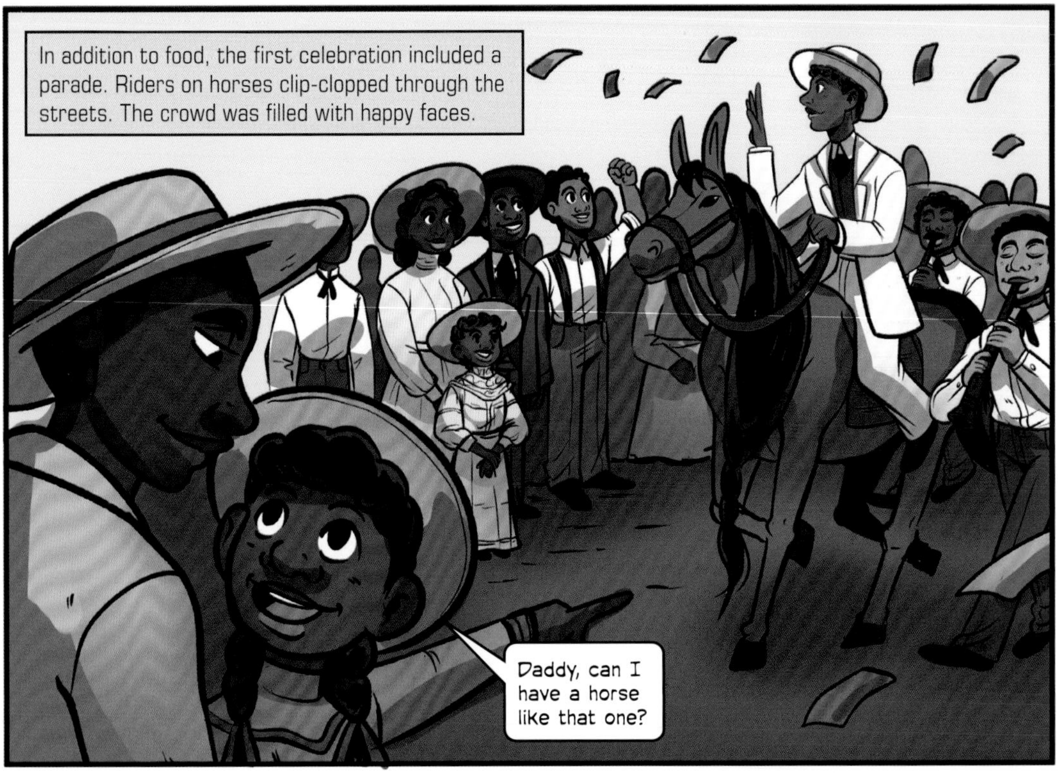
In addition to food, the first celebration included a parade. Riders on horses clip-clopped through the streets. The crowd was filled with happy faces.
Daddy, can I have a horse like that one?

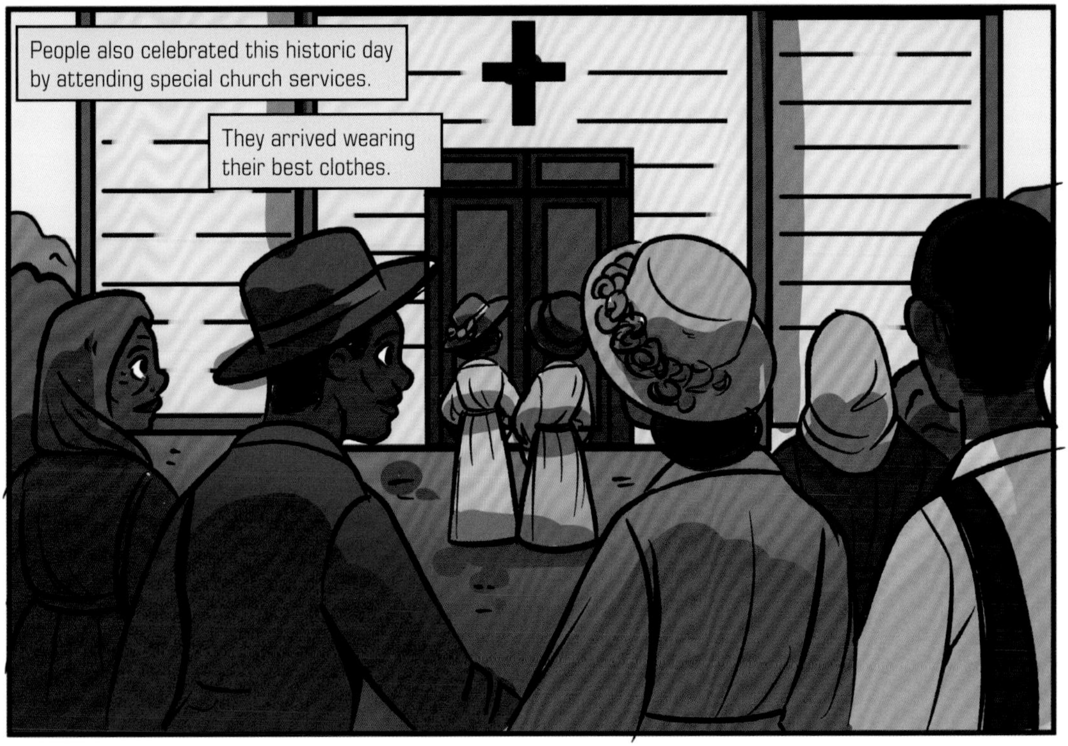
People also celebrated this historic day by attending special church services.
They arrived wearing their best clothes.

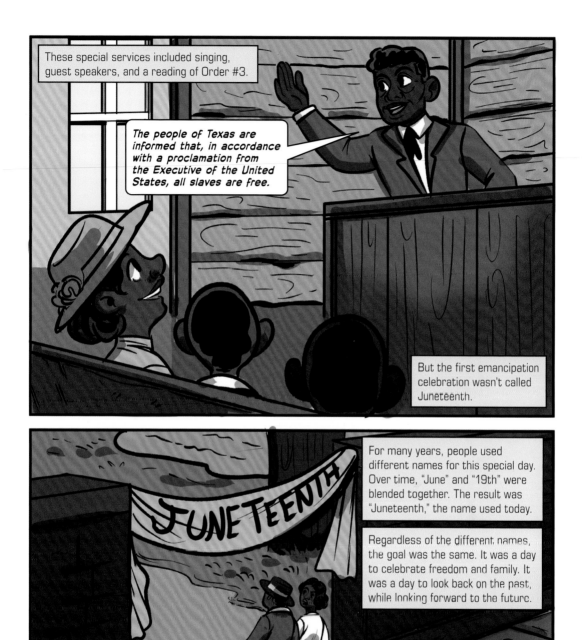

These special services included singing, guest speakers, and a reading of Order #3.

The people of Texas are informed that, in accordance with a proclamation from the Executive of the United States, all slaves are free.

But the first emancipation celebration wasn't called Juneteenth.

For many years, people used different names for this special day. Over time, "June" and "19th" were blended together. The result was "Juneteenth," the name used today.

Regardless of the different names, the goal was the same. It was a day to celebrate freedom and family. It was a day to look back on the past, while looking forward to the future.

Chapter 3 Juneteenth Evolves

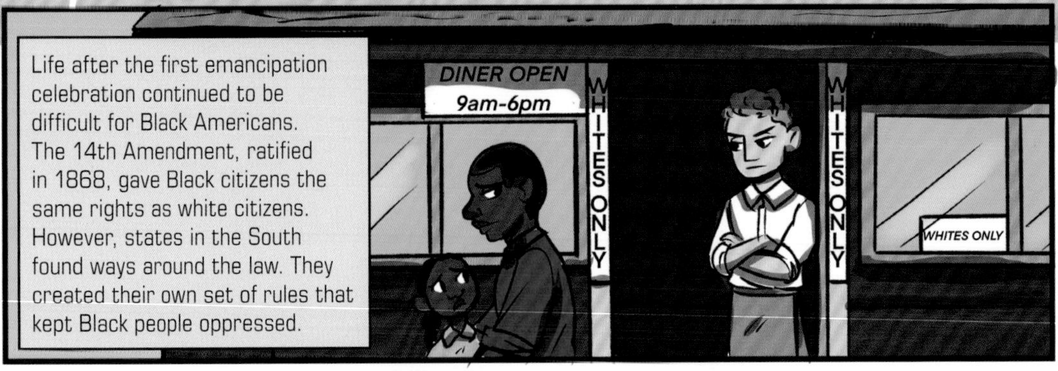
Life after the first emancipation celebration continued to be difficult for Black Americans. The 14th Amendment, ratified in 1868, gave Black citizens the same rights as white citizens. However, states in the South found ways around the law. They created their own set of rules that kept Black people oppressed.
DINER OPEN
9am-6pm
WHITES ONLY
WHITES ONLY
WHITES ONLY

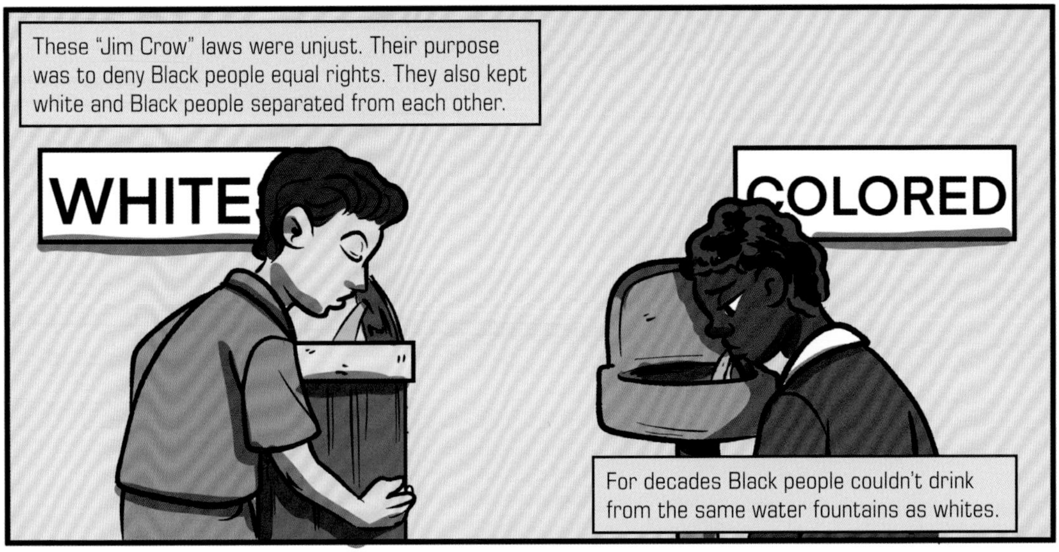
These "Jim Crow" laws were unjust. Their purpose was to deny Black people equal rights. They also kept white and Black people separated from each other.
WHITE
COLORED
For decades Black people couldn't drink from the same water fountains as whites.

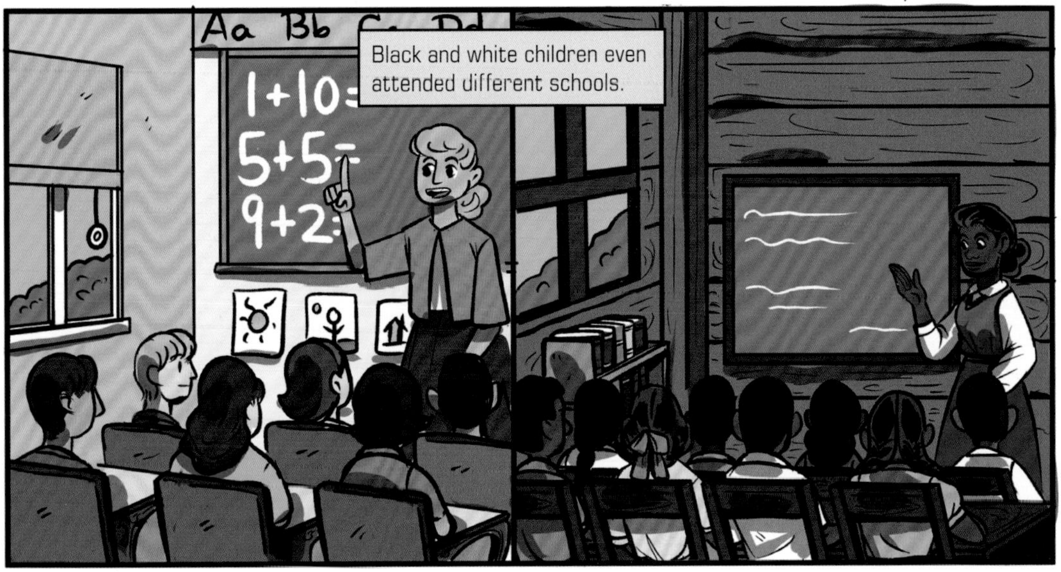
Black and white children even attended different schools.
1+10=
5+5=
9+2=

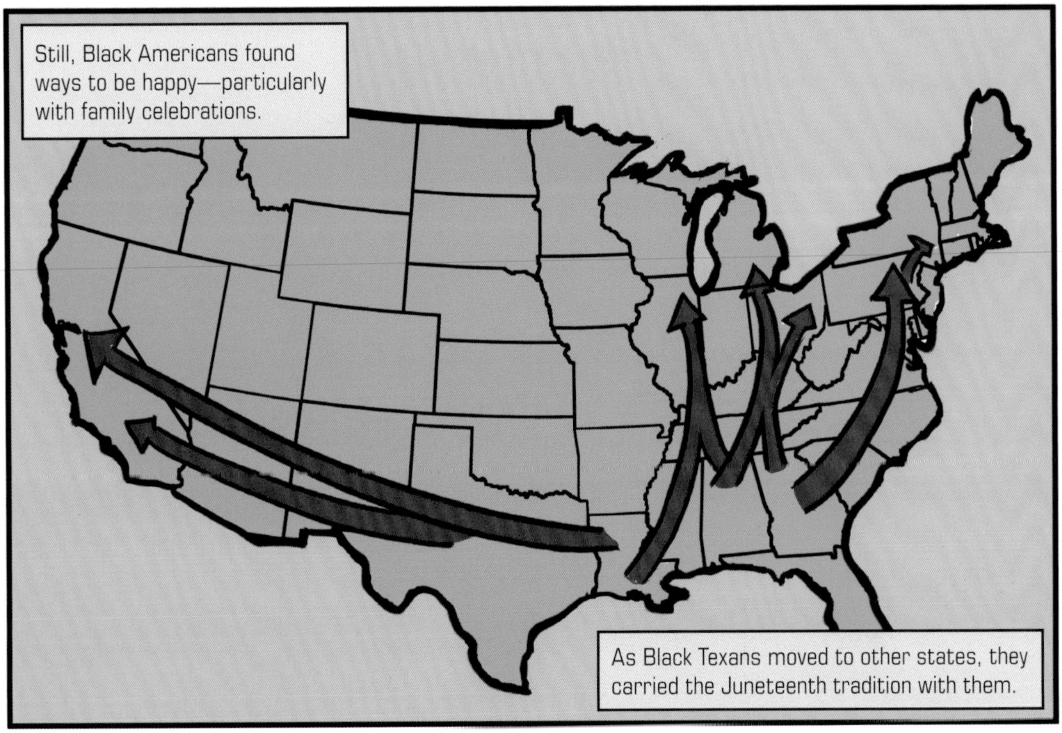
Still, Black Americans found ways to be happy—particularly with family celebrations.
As Black Texans moved to other states, they carried the Juneteenth tradition with them.

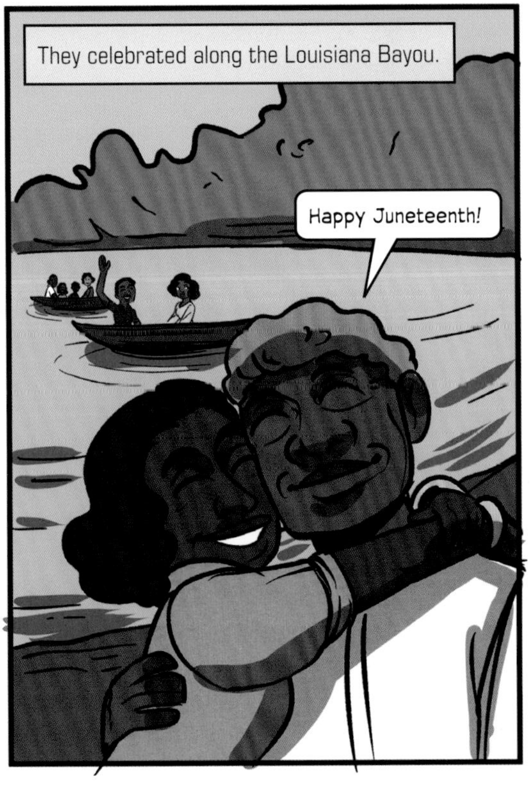
They celebrated along the Louisiana Bayou.
Happy Juneteenth!

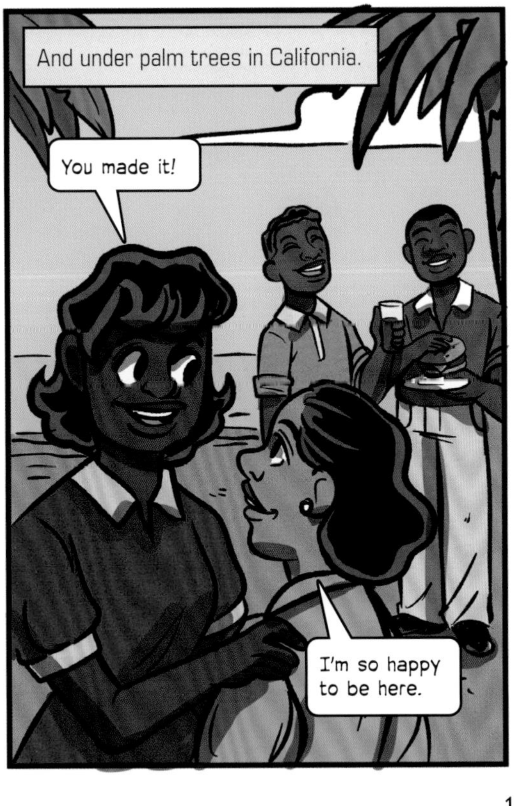
And under palm trees in California.
You made it!
I'm so happy to be here.

But as the years went by, keeping the Juneteenth tradition going proved difficult. It didn't help that the holiday wasn't officially recognized by any states or the U.S. government. That made it challenging for Black people to honor this special day.

I'd like to take the day off to celebrate Juneteenth.

That's not a holiday.

It was also difficult—if not impossible—for Black people to rent event halls and other spaces to hold their celebrations.

EVENT

Inquire Inside

HALL

We Only Rent to Whites

Still, some Black Americans refused to give up on Juneteenth.

That land became Emancipation Park and was used to host Juneteenth events thereafter.

In 1872, Reverend Jack Yates raised $1,000 to purchase 10 acres of land in Houston, Texas.

The holiday faced even more obstacles in the early 1900s.

EMANCIPATION PROCLAMATION

In classrooms, teachers focused more on Lincoln's Emancipation Proclamation as the end of slavery than on Granger's arrival in Galveston. Sadly, Juneteenth's popularity began to fade.

In addition, as Black elders died, so did many of their Juneteenth stories and traditions.

Grandpop, what's your favorite part of Juneteenth?

Your grandma's good cooking, of course!

Mine too!

While celebrations continued in some families, they disappeared in others.

Interest in Juneteenth continued to decline until a tragedy near the end of the Civil Rights Movement.

Everyone deserves to be treated equally.

The Civil Rights Movement was a campaign to end racial discrimination and a fight for equal rights for Black Americans. It took place during the 1950s and 1960s.

One of its most prominent leaders was Dr. Martin Luther King Jr. Dr. King was a Baptist minister and Civil Rights activist.

Throughout the movement, Dr. King led marches and staged sit-ins at restaurants that refused to serve Black patrons. He always believed the protests should be nonviolent.

In 1967, Dr. King planned the Poor People's Campaign. He wanted people of all races and income levels to march together.

The goal was to demand that Congress act to help poor people in the United States. The events were scheduled to take place starting in May 1968.

We're going to march on Washington, D.C.

Then tragedy struck. Dr. King was assassinated on April 4, 1968, in Memphis, Tennessee.

Dr. King's death stunned the world. But his fellow Civil Rights leaders vowed to continue the fight for freedom and equality. One of them was Reverend Ralph Abernathy.

We must finish the work Dr. King started and carry on with the Poor People's Campaign!

One of the campaign's main events was the Solidarity Day Rally, which was held on June 19. More than 50,000 people attended.

One hundred three years ago, the last enslaved Texans found out they were free. Yet, the struggle for racial equality continues.

After the rally, participants returned to their own communities. Many brought the Juneteenth tradition back to life.

In cities across the country, Juneteenth events became popular again. Milwaukee, Wisconsin, and Minneapolis, Minnesota, were two of the earliest cities to hold events. Celebrations in these cities are still going strong today.

With renewed interest in Juneteenth, some politicians started pushing to make the day an official state holiday. In February 1979, Texas state representative Al Edwards introduced a bill to the Texas House of Representatives.

The time has come to finally give Juneteenth the recognition it deserves. Join with me in voting yes to making Juneteenth a state holiday.

Then, on June 7, 1979, Texas Governor William P. Clements signed the bill into law. It took effect January 1, 1980.

The next summer, the state began sponsoring Juneteenth events. In addition, people who worked for the state government got the day off with pay. Some cities held special events, and some businesses closed.

After Texas, other states—including Massachusetts, New York, Virginia, Washington, and Oregon—began observing Juneteenth too. But none of them made it an official state holiday.

In fact, it would take decades before any other states adopted Juneteenth as an official state holiday. Virginia did so in 2020. Other states soon followed, including Louisiana, Maine, and Utah.

In February 2022, South Dakota became the last state to recognize Juneteenth as a holiday or observance.

Meanwhile, people began asking the government to make Juneteenth a federal holiday. On federal holidays, such as Christmas Day, July 4th, and Dr. Martin Luther King Jr. Day, people who work for the federal government get the day off with pay. Most state employees have the day off too.

One of the important campaigners for making Juneteenth a federal holiday was Ms. Opal Lee from Fort Worth, Texas. Lee, a retired teacher and community activist, has been called "the grandmother of Juneteenth."

I want to discuss with you why Juneteenth has not been made a national holiday. . . . To that end I'm planning to walk to Washington, D.C., to hear from you for myself the reason why.

After working to keep Juneteenth alive for decades, she wrote a letter to President Barack Obama in 2016.

If I can do ten miles a day, it will take 21 days to get to the White House

Lee was 89 years old at the time. Still, she initially planned to walk from her home to Washington, D.C.

Lee's journey to Washington, D.C., began on September 1, 2016.

Instead of walking the whole way there, she traveled to different cities and held 2.5-mile (4-kilometer) walks in each one. These miles represented the 2.5 years it took General Granger to reach Galveston.

Along the way, Lee asked people to sign her petition to make Juneteenth a federal holiday.

We need 100,000 signatures to present to Congress.

In January 2017, Lee finally arrived in Washington, D.C. She couldn't meet with the president because he was out of town, but that didn't stop her. She continued walking in support of Juneteenth for the next several years.

I refuse to let the efforts we've made die on the vine.

Then, in September 2020, Lee delivered her petition to Congress. It had 1.5 million signatures!

On June 16, 2021, the hard work of Lee and others paid off. The U.S. Senate passed a bill to make Juneteenth a federal holiday. The next day, the bill passed in the U.S. House of Representatives.

President Joe Biden signed the bill into law on June 17. The next day—because June 19 fell on a Saturday—Juneteenth was observed as a federal holiday for the very first time.

By making Juneteenth a federal holiday, all Americans can feel the power of this day, and learn from our history, and celebrate progress . . .

WOW! I'm so excited to see my lifelong mission of making Juneteenth a national holiday become reality.

Becoming a federal holiday was a huge milestone for Juneteenth. It recognized how important the holiday is to Black Americans. It also invited people of all races to learn about and celebrate an important part of U.S. history.

JUNETEENTH

In the few short years since becoming a federal holiday, events on and around the holiday have become bigger and more widespread.

Still, some things about the holiday haven't changed.

There's great music—and of course, tasty food.

Juneteenth continues to be a time to celebrate with family and friends.

Special church services are still held, and a reading of Order #3 is still on the program.

And while we shouldn't forget past injustices, Juneteenth also celebrates our country's freedom to move forward. This holiday honors the millions of Black Americans who lost their lives while enslaved. It celebrates those who survived the hardships of slavery until dreams of freedom became a reality. And it's a reminder that even in the darkest times, a brighter future is on the horizon.

MORE ABOUT JUNETEENTH

- General Granger didn't arrive in Galveston, Texas, alone. He was accompanied by more than 2,000 Union soldiers. Granger was in Texas to not only read the order, but to take back control of the state from the Confederacy. The soldiers were there to ensure a peaceful transition.

- General Granger and his troops read and posted the order at several different locations including churches, the courthouse, and other government buildings around Galveston.

- General Order #3 asked the enslaved not to immediately leave the plantations. Instead, it suggested they stay and work for wages. Of course, many enslaved people left as soon as Granger finished reading the order.

- Since 1997, Juneteenth has had its own flag. The flag is blue at the top and red at the bottom with a white star in the center.

- Juneteenth is the oldest African American holiday in the United States.

- For some, Juneteenth is celebrated longer than the actual day. Events may take place over a few days, a week, or the entire month of June.

- One of the largest Juneteenth events took place after George Floyd's death in May 2020. Floyd was a Black man murdered by a white police officer in Minneapolis. Less than one month later, millions of people across the country marched on Juneteenth to seek justice for Floyd and bring awareness to what happened.

GLOSSARY

abolish (uh-BOL-ish)—to put an end to something officially

accordance (uh-KORD-uhnss)—to be in agreement with something, especially a rule

activist (AK-tih-vist)—someone who works for political or social change

emancipation (i-MAN-si-pay-shuhn)—freedom from enslavement or control

executive (ig-ZEK-yuh-tiv)—having to do with the branch of government that makes sure the laws are obeyed

military (MIL-uh-tair-ee)—the armed forces of a state or country

oppressed (oh-PREST)—treated in a cruel, unjust, and hard way

petition (puh-TISH-uhn)—a letter signed by many people asking leaders for a change

proclamation (prah-cluh-MAY-shuhn)—a public announcement or statement

ratified (RAT-uh-fide)—formally approved

sharecropping (SHAIR-krop-ing)—to rent a plot of land for farming by paying the owner in crops instead of cash

tragedy (TRAJ-uh-dee)—a very sad event

READ MORE

Duncan, Alice Faye. *Opal Lee and What It Means to Be Free: The True Story of the Grandmother of Juneteenth.* Nashville: Thomas Nelson, 2021.

Sabelko, Rebecca. *Juneteenth.* Minneapolis: Bellwether Media, Inc., 2023.

Wyeth, Sharon Dennis. *Juneteenth: Our Day of Freedom.* New York: Random House Children's Books, 2022.

INTERNET SITES

GovInfo: Juneteenth
govinfo.gov/features/juneteenth

National Park Service: Juneteenth: A Celebration of Freedom
nps.gov/articles/juneteenth-origins.htm

Time for Kids: A Juneteenth Celebration
timeforkids.com/g56/a-juneteenth-celebration

ABOUT THE AUTHOR

Myra Faye Turner is a poet and author based in New Orleans. She has written for grown-ups but prefers writing for young readers. She has written more than two dozen fiction and nonfiction books for children and young adults, covering diverse topics like politics, the Apollo moon landing, edible insects, Black history, U.S. history, and science. When she's not writing, she spends her days reading, napping, playing Wordle, and drinking coffee.

photo by Myra Faye Turner

ABOUT THE ILLUSTRATOR

Markia Jenai was raised in Detroit, Michigan, during rough times but found adventure through art, drawing, and storytelling. Those interests led her to study at the Academy of Art University in San Francisco, California. An avid lover of fantasy settings, cultures, and mythology, Markia has made it her goal to create worlds where people of color are front and center. Diversity within her art means the world to her, and she dreams of the day when everyone will see themselves in media and have the same access to telling their own stories.

photo by Markia Jenai